In June the Labyrinth

In June the Labyrinth

Cynthia Hogue

poems

Red Hen Press | *Pasadena, CA*

Book layout by Sarah Wong
Hand lettering by Cassidy Trier

Names: Hogue, Cynthia, author.
Title: In June the labyrinth / Cynthia Hogue.
Description: Pasadena, CA : Red Hen Press, [2017]
Identifiers: LCCN 2016048404 | ISBN 9781597090377 (pbk. : alk. paper)
Classification: LCC PS3558.O34754 A6 2017 | DDC 811/.54—dc23
LC record available at https://lccn.loc.gov/2016048404

The National Endowment for the Arts, the Los Angeles County Arts Commission, the
Dwight Stuart Youth Fund, the Max Factor Family Foundation, the Pasadena Tournament
of Roses Foundation, the Pasadena Arts & Culture Commission and the City of Pasadena
Cultural Affairs Division, the City of Los Angeles Department of Cultural Affairs, the
Audrey & Sydney Irmas Charitable Foundation, Sony Pictures Entertainment, Amazon
Literary Partnership, and the Sherwood Foundation partially support Red Hen Press.

First Edition
Published by Red Hen Press
www.redhen.org

ACKNOWLEDGMENTS

Thanks to the editors of the following journals, anthologies, and special issues for publishing individual poems (sometimes with different titles and in earlier versions): *Bosque*: ("a journey"), ("believing belief"), ("*still* her"), ("the field"); *Hinchas de Poesia*: ("I could still call Elle"), ("the green way"), ("thinking of *you*") ; *Hotel Amerika*: ("the labyrinth of honestly") under the title "the lake of honestly"; *Plume*: ("the wayfarer"), ("to label something something") in a composite poem including ("a spire"), ("the keep") and ("well being"), ("to walk the labyrinth is amazing"); *TAB*: ("L is for love") under the title "Then Became"; *Third Coast*: ("the boulder"), ("verge") in earlier, untitled versions; *Tupelo Quarterly*: ("Elle in hospice"), ("in time"), ("my particular"); *Wordgathering: A Journal of Disability Poetry and Literature*: ("alone in love"), ("curtains of darkness"), ("the labyrinth of forgiveness"); *Zócalo Magazine*: ("the labyrinth's experience").

("Elle's *good*") was included in *In Like Company: The Salt River Review & Porch Anthology*, edited by James Cervantes (MadHat Press, 2015); ("still herself") was included in the fiftieth anniversary edition of *Puerto del Sol* (2015), edited by Carmen Giménez Smith; ("the unwritten volume") was published under the title "The Unwritten Volume" in *Prairie Schooner* in the special section "Women and the Global Imagination," guest-edited by Alicia Ostriker (Winter 2014), and included in *Best American Poetry* (2016), edited by Edward Hirsch.

Deep thanks to Wendy Barker, Martha Collins, and Alicia Ostriker for your generous words and abiding support; to the Helene M. Wurlitzer Foundation of New Mexico for a quiet space in which to begin this book before I knew it was one; to the English Department and the Creative Writing Program at Arizona State University for the leave time that enabled me to advance this project; to my CW colleagues for so generously covering for me—especially Norman Dubie, Sally Ball, and Alberto Ríos; to the Maxine and Jonathan Marshall Chair in Modern and Contemporary Poetry for the resources to undertake travel necessary to the writing of these poems; and to the MFA Program at Cornell University for the invitation to be Distinguished Visiting Writer in the Spring of 2014, during which time I had the peace of mind conducive to going deeply into and completing the project in draft. My thanks to everyone in English at Cornell for their warm welcome, in particular Alice Fulton, Lyrae Van Clief-Stefanon, Ishion Hutchinson, and Valzhyna Mort. To Martha Collins, Alan Michael Parker, Lois Roma-Deeley, and Jeannine Savard, all of whom beneficently read the whole manuscript and gave me judicious feedback: you gave me the gift of your expertise and friendship, and you gave me courage. To Kate Gale and Mark Cull of Red Hen Press: Ever-thanks for standing by me, and for the beautiful books you make. To the friends and family (especially my adored husband, Sylvain Gallais) who journeyed with me to walk labyrinths, although they wished many times to be doing something else, *ever-love*.

In memory of L. W., A. O., M. M., and L. E. H.,

"holy strong ones"

CONTENTS

I

II

III

IV

In June the Labyrinth

[The] narrative is genealogical but it does not simply amount to an act of memory. It witnesses, *in the manner of an ethical or political act, for today and for tomorrow.*

—Jacques Derrida, *The Gift of Death*

The purpose which guided [her] was not impossible, though it was supernatural.

—Jorge Luis Borges, *Labyrinths*

I

*F's gift from his rose garden and the rosette in the labyrinth's
center like a premise. A promise: the real rose closed tight,
stuck as an afterthought in a glass of water, which, overnight,
opened. As if the window's sash were up. Everything perfumed.*

("a journey")

Elle, ill, prayed for a miracle I did not know but
dreamed she'd go & forth went without obstacle.

To journey to the labyrinth,
hours through hilly countryside and village,
like nothing I remembered,

spires rising in a golden wheat field:
possibly a photograph or film,
my mind not recalling the source,

the image gaining heft in thought,
but from the car, train tracks, tree alleys.
All signs overhead.

In the town, we couldn't find
the cathedral with the labyrinth,
though houses were low, of ancient wood,

slightly aslant, and crooked, weathered overhangs
for (old times) slops.
A few cobbled streets.

We were hungry and ate.
Your lips smacked between bites,
and I dabbed my mouth often.

Then it was there.

("a troth")

a town satellites around its sacred structures,

– "on a little rise in the square" –

tourist shops, selling icons, flutter with cards,

– "the most important site of marian pilgrimage" –

local legends, labyrinth bijoux (though I'm not here

– "thanne longen folk to seken straunge strondes" –

to window-shop but to wager my words for a life)

– *"vierge aux miracles comme vous"* –

("the unwritten volume")

Elle's writing her book of wisdom.
She writes until she cannot hold her pen.
The labyrinth miraculously is uncovered.

An American woman's progressing on her knees.
She read something but not Elle's book.
No one will read Elle's book.

I walk the circular path, first the left side,
then the right, casting petals to the north,
east, south, and west (this intuitively).

A diminutive prelate shoos me away.
When he leaves, I return to the center.
The organist, practicing, strikes up *Phantom*.

Elle says she cannot hear him.
Elle! I cry, *I cannot* see *you.*
I had prayed Death spare you.

Remember our meal among the termites
of Arcadia Street, that cottage of spirits
with its riddled beams and long veranda

bordered by plantain trees, and the spiral
you traced for me on scrap-paper?
I kept it for such a long time.

The organist, of course, is playing Bach.
A boy has scattered the petals I threw.
Elle's voice surrounds me.

To quiet hills I lift mine eyes.

("L is for love")

Elle fell at first touch
Lazy the long
      And breezy sunlight \ mingling ==

Hours measured in
Summer's cicada's thrumming
      The heart's vast and cratered purpose ==

Union of weighted, the rooted
      and fulcrum == Spread out
like wild thyme, heal-all, forget-me-not

Love's accident's
glittering wand waves == hosts ==
      the delicate-eyed \ the dowering

("the labyrinth of honestly")

have you ever with-
held something in
case it'd hurt someone?

Elle asked. Though truth
hurt why don't
you try it? exactly

what's *love* got
to do with your *life* –
do you know can you see

what I mean? now
here's the hard part: ·
you're on an island

named Labyrinth:
what do you do? take
the hand out-held for help?

dissociate, hunch up,
step over the stones and
walk away,

or whisper words you never meant
heard?
honestly you lied to hide

all that truth dis-
plays so nothing, no one
reached you: *isn't that true?*

("safely")

The tall man with a long neck
who loved Elle's voice
was frightened the fuck

out of his mind by Elle herself,
who tried one last time with
the demon of worldly goods.

Let me get this
straight: I'm to give
up everything for you?

"Things, C, just things."
Elle made observations
in ways that rendered choices

self-evident. The simple facts
proved eloquent: his terrified
midlife lay in

deed: a small-hearted
man quickly crossing
back to *safely.*

("a mazing")

Missing him she made
of her garden a maze
which she called *labyrinth*.

Mazes aren't labyrinths
though often confused with them.
Only one is for pilgrimage.

The other's a game.
Fearless Elle never spared
herself. The journey was all

she saw,
until her lover, her *daimon*:
gamed her garden.

("my pilgrimage")

A pilgrim necessarily

"leaves home voluntarily"

to become the *"nomade illuminé"*

a wanderer "ex patria (*'sans terroir propre'*)"

In legend rarely a woman,

who instead sits (visibly) by the window

embroidering with the others

old wives' tales in one of which

Elle is writing furiously at her desk

on her long-envisioned quest

to complete her book

Her cat purrs by the keyboard

and her cold persists

She, already shadowed by the Angel,

whom she sees clearly

hovering (inversed) to her

                    left

("believing belief")

I was not thinking of her I was trying not to think of her.
I left a cold place and traveled to the warm it was raining
the hard rain down that fell into a rata-tat-tat on the wings
as I deplaned. *I love the rain*, I said, but it was not true.
Rain's gloomy and I was glad. Elle was still alive and I
believed belief could heal her. I had a dream in which
someone died and when I woke I thought, Someone has died.
I hardly knew death was so sudden. Before Elle saw the
doctor, she had something and then she had something else.
After she saw the doctor it was diagnosed as something
worse. *Elle oh Elle*, I said when word reached me. And,
Oh no. Who doesn't say something that isn't anything?

("my particular")

Seeking succor
I traveled your pilgrim's course
ignorantly, coincidentally as

impenitent, unbeliever,
but guided, as if you,
far away in your particular desert,

could be saved by a few words
said *right* –
(Of a *route*: direct.

Obs. OE and ME *fitting*,
leading to uncertainty as to
which meaning is intended ...) –

Oh, I lit the candle
that I paid a coin for
and knelt at the small icon

carved of the dark wood of a pear tree,
with embroidered gold-filigreed
vestments. Anyway: prayed.

("and to see")

- Elle waited for a "cure"
- "sometimes water and sometimes a ring of fire"
- "Love, that of erth and se hath governaunce"
- "To reinforce this important feminine aspect"
- "What little of Elle's life was *left*"
- (*left*, from OE *lef,* weak, and AS *lyft,* broken)

("**in time**")

Sage Elle in her last travail.
To be beyond hope
is to happen into a most spacious

sensibility at the very moment
of greatest need.
To be outside

the confines of desire is to arrest
time, which devours space,
insatiable, immeasurable.

II

("*dehors* et *dedans*")

Outside *is* inside,
I misread Bachelard's French,
imagining Elle belonging when

life's excluding her.
She will message me,
I think. But I cannot harbor

her. She is inside herself,
sliced from unreal, *real,*
as *no* from *not.*

("to label something something")

There was an ancient well-site beneath the labyrinth
I did not reach, the part underground,
labeled (what else?) The Crypt.

But labels always hide something
about what they seem to define.
They set the thing apart

without disclosing why.
Alive costs a pretty penny
to see The Crypt now.

("well being")

There an ancient grotto's been
blocked up to quell "miraculous waters" in
the "magical cave";
how concrete's the desiccate source,
the *well*-being.

("the keep")

No archeological dig. No label
explaining who'd built what or when,
who'd come, and who'd destroyed

the Guardian of the Underworld,
as she was called. Or, is called.
Unblocked of late, her spring has not

sprung back. A guide will not say that.
The label kept me out,
and from Elle's ken.

("the thinking veiling")

I read in
        another time
                that "the house"
counters the "demons
        of space in the universe."
                Bold Elle, well,
burned through space-
        demons like karma,
                floated from one
abode to another
        without possession
                because, in fact,
she carried her house
        like a shell around her,
                framed in that whorled
and wieldy doorway.
        You can simply
                step out from
the thinking veiling
        the truth, C, and
                then you'll see.

("high plains drifter")

I didn't listen.
        I mulled,
                muddled, forgot,
journeyed to fabled
        source of
                magic earth,
ate the mythic
        mud and did
                not heal
or heed
        her the oracle
                orienting me
toward change
        like a charm-
                less spell.
Elle, herself,
        drifted to the
                high plains.

("I could still call Elle")

I woke with foreboding—the feeling not dispelled with waking—
and rose to catch the full moon dead center of a blue, oval window
made by foliage in the woods. The setting so fleeting I stilled to
watch. I fought fear who once had none. Coward, I said, afraid.
No one gathered the small, wild apples stippling the ground. The
moon, a white owl flying off. The dream was I was thinking fear-
lessly.

("about face")

About love, she was never
        right, but danger:
                never wrong.
I was in danger from Y,
        something under-
                ground, C,
your cellar (your unc.),
        flooding, the door
                permeable,
indefensible. In dreams
        I was smothered by Y,
                who actually
was hiding all
        day like a snake
                in the garden maze
until nightfall
        when he'd sneak in
                to eat. Calling Elle
at last I heard. *Easy,*
        C: Just change
                the locks.

("Elle tells")

Only for you will I finish a story
that keeps you on edge,   *(boundary*
holding your ring finger,
watching my hands curve and –

swans on a pond – arms rise   *presumed, exposed:*
and open as in embrace.
Touched? Here are
some air kisses:

Smooch. Smooch.
Before you, the city's dark.
Streets wind labyrin-
thine. Now go home: *not only more pointed but*

the place in which (I know)
you feel in danger,
for words, fear-full, wound.
I say, *Change that.*   *impermanent:)*

("a spire")

To confer a form on space

To consider the function

To cast space like a sculpture

or fix clothespins on shaves of wood

so they curve around,

usefully shaping the space for sound

(from strings or a pipe through which wind)

To soar into a tower the exact height

of the nave's length, the one pointing

to sun or moon (depending),

the other toward the altar,

and beyond, the horizon

visible from the spire,

and the spire seen from anywhere:

the unstable hierarchy of proportions

the geometry of which has not sufficiently

("to be-frend")

- (Defense of) ≠ (Connect to)
- Fortified in the house: "*la femme à la fenêtre*"
- "the most poetical topic in the world" –
- Here's freedom, C ≤ ONE'S OWN ROOM ≥
- *good frend, I'll lock you out* –

("to walk the labyrinth is amazing")

Everything looped, spiraled, circular (thought)
But the labyrinth's not a maze but a singular way
to strike "the profoundest chord"
across aspire

Those who enter the labyrinth can leave
(pilgrims sometimes don't)
(Elle did not)
Inside the largest circle

(the labyrinth itself)
splits into equal parts
(demi-arcs or waves)
No, silly, Elle whispers, *petals*

> *If measured through the centre of the petals there should be two parts for each*
> *petal and one for the entry, but calculations from the measurements show that*
> *this is not so. The difference is about ½". There is no way around this problem.*

We must seek a solution
to the geometry of petals,
the consequential mystery
of Elle's message:

I was sick and am not
healed.   I am not blind
but dead.   I am not dead
but silenced.   Alone, in love.

III

("peace, love")

Elle, belle, sought a Love
which still "rules the sky"
"of your heart" (yes *you*!).

Found the road long
and time short
as a holy strong one.

Found the "labyrinth of tangled arguments"
fear-filled demons used to counter
Love's "sweet peace."

("alone in love")

I was trying to recall that
those who enter the labyrinth
can leave.

Calculations from the measurements show
this is not so.
There's no way around this problem.

I must seek a solution to the geometry
that my future has unverged with yours.
I am not dead but silenced.

("like to a sphere")

Love of sea and land
sufficed. *You*:
the demon she forgave in the end.

Thought of your betrayal
even to the point of madness.
Worried it through like a rope.

"likewise God"
"and of happiness"
"didst teach that"

"paradise might be called"
"a labyrinth rather"
"than a garden"

"In body like to a sphere on all sides perfectly rounded"

("**thinking of** *you*")

When *you* aren't here
and I call *you* to mind,
can *you* hear me?

I conjure a character flush
with flesh, your name as
sign of your life apart,

but have no sense
of whom I address.
Let me ask *you*: who who who?

Looking for *you*,
I wander through a dark wood,
a grove, a crowd

of trees, so many I at last
give *you* world's *enough*,
time never to be found:

Can *you* then see
that giving another something—
let's say *you* these hours among trees

with the space they need
to make the poison choking us
into a potion healing all—

is an example of the gift with no
strings, though *you* may think
there will always be strings?

("verge")

Elle says: "Understand when I see in"
"the future I mention the future"
"in order to propose constructing"
"a labyrinth I call Crystal,"
"along a park signifying eternity, or"

"the timeless stream."

"What I mean to say is paradise,"
"but let's speak for the moment"
"of a garden the edges of which"
"are geometric or even"
"labyrinthine. Grass verges"
"punctuate the straight lines and"

"loops of"

"this deliberately unverdured space,"
"as in": *My future has unverged with yours.*
You have no foresight only facts,
and no vision only verdure.
"For the moment Elle's by a high wall"
"that looks out over the labyrinth."

("the crux")

Elle calls and demon answers.
She thinks she knows his name.
This is the crux of her belief:
No one here to fall
back on but herself, she the wild,
and true blue, the only starry night.

She wakes to *his* face and scent.
If he touched her would she fly?
Turn fearsome angel batting wings
about his ears, flitting in his thoughts
as if to stay? She calls once more:
Go home.

There is no further object or objection.
No sin or sinisterness. She'll walk
the labyrinth meekly above ground
(there is a clearing in her heart). A crunching sound
like wheels on gravel, a whirring
as of flight. A lifetime's surrender.

("symbolic")

Once upon a pallid lake
over supper on a breezy patio,
I mused to Elle, "The roundness
of the labyrinth's form
comes from the cunt,
the rosy opening of the vagina,
connoting birth." Skeptic Elle:

Where did you read that?
I stammered, vague, "Goddess studies"
(which I hadn't studied),
or some such stuff I had.
Quiet, vehement voice:
I don't believe you.
The wind rose over the vast lake.

How had I known
(how does one *know*
the meaning of a symbol)?
Ethical Elle, you always questioned
facile claims to knowing
without proof, to keep
your thinking free.

("cunning")

- "not a maze, but a single way" [and]

- "not a mindless trick but an ordered track" [—]

- "from *labrus* a thing to be held" [or]

- "*lapis* the thing to seek" [in]

- "the world we live in" [but]

- "let us approach the problem in another way" [if]

- "the cunt we come from" [is]

- "the unthinkable" [then]

- "think: *cunn, cunnen* ME, coming to know" [:]

- "first to know, and then to see"

("Elle in hospice")

Saturday we spoke of stopping hydration.
Elle asked us to *just shoot me or make me
well.* We were her agents of change,
we strangers from afar. Monday
the morphine drip. Or maybe Sunday.
The on-call hospice nurse had the worst
tobacco and whiskey voice and the voice
upset Elle who roused at last to say, No more
love. But the nurse in the middle of her
story continued so bent on telling the whole
she forgot the point of being there at all.
We heard her though we no longer listened,
having turned to Elle whose
breathing had begun to quicken.

("the labyrinth's experience")

take shoes.   collect yourself.   sit.
[if weather permits the ground is a rewarding experience.]

think of different people as you.
pay attention as they rise and then let them go.

                                        get centered.

there are many ways of asking,
two of which are: how am I loved? how do I love?

I am a teacher.   let me teach you
—often startling—

some feel a sense of confusion
as they remember there is only one path in and one path out,

but you will not get lost.
you will feel lost.

set your own pace and pattern
here

- all thoughts go   **[attention]**
- with a listening heart.   **[question]**
- repeat over and over: **[repetition]**
- *all thoughts go with a listening heart all thoughts go with a listening heart*
- to pray   **[petition]**
- as your body wishes

[raise arms and move legs]

                [bend torso and sway hips]

("still herself")

The difference between finding a way
and finding the way

is like that between not knowing
and having forgotten:

Elle trying to tell who's leaning close
to kiss her brow

with its mounded wen at the scalp line
she'd had from a fall at ten,

the bangs she wore all her life
to hide it, cut at the time with such care

by Mother, and misrecognizing.
Mother, she cries.

She's begun her journey,
they have come to us to say

instead of *She's dying*.
The sun is a balm.

We stranger this light.
Elle's still, pilgrimly, herself.

("the green way")

Street glistens with dim, watery light,

        some of the stones dark with dew,

        others gray

or rose. Elle walks this every day.

The river is high at the moment.

The foot of the road has flooded.

        Elle passes the yellow house

        with green shutters, its yard

of Queen Anne's lace, paintbrush,

        the bluebells and bleeding hearts

        strung like pennants, and turns

because she feels warmth from early sun

        on her face. Her patent leather shoes

        still new for school. Their shine attracts

her gaze. The way she knows to walk

on her own is past the cemetery,

the small, unpainted houses

           among the trees, green with June.

IV

("the bitter")

Here ends the year in Hell
I suffered that you all
be forgiven your sins, says Elle,
who feels this wholly,
and speaks so calmly as well
as bitterly, bitterly herself
so grievously hopeful

until she can no longer tell
the hour or her name. *O world,*
I cannot hold
you anymore! World, world,
here such a passion was as filled
me to overflowing, murmurs Elle,
who'd been so fiercely hopeful.

("the boulder")

I woke when Elle, ill,
down the hill in hospital,
spoke to me. *Now are you after all
this with your mother?* I called

to myself. Outside, dark still.
Something like a boulder in the grass.
A ripple of supple surface.
No other movement until a streetlight

caught huge antlers from above,
the dawn roebuck lifting his head to look.
I stood at the foot of the stairs,
deciding whether to go out

in the dark night to her side
the morning Elle died.

("the field")

Dream of two white eagles circling above us
in great helices (meaning
what? I ask). *C, Elle says, no ideas*

but in dreams.
No connection but in this field of
associations, tendered, for example.

("the rose")

the ground of the labyrinth
which deeply
and to inspire

Elle treads the spirals the cross
of which various schools of thought
have thought predated X

thus when she carries the rose
quartz heart that
warmed in her hand

is beating in time
she starts
to sing her

                    heart out

("Elle muses")

Alone.

Alone, love.

Love, alone.

Elle as maid, bride, *mère*
and crone (*never really
reached really*).

Elle, alone.

Alone, Elle

found anew

her "magic,"
the "marvel" of the word,
her pilgrimage to

feel

love alone, of all else,

remaining.

World's largesse. Chalice full:
*Love all
one.*

("Elle's *good*")

The cumulation of experience sufficient
to change heart
is the distinction between discovering
a space one has made,
a being one became,
and having refused. Elle reached
for moral limits to exceed them,
a "finisterre," a cliff:

if she leaped, was she more
or less moral? She loved from afar,
way, way from the bottom
of her heart, that sheer
drop down, down, she fell
in love. Then space estranged.
The strangeness could not—
there was nothing she could do—

grow familiar again. Now no time's
left to try something else, something
other than, though new perceptions
intervene, complicate what is simply
the essential morality of goodness:
Are you a good *woman?*
Elle was asked by a stranger, alone,
at breakfast in a little *pensione*.

Moral Elle, speaking truth to
an intruder on her solitude
(*I try to be*), surprised by
the force of the kiss, fought, won:
being close enough to touch
differed from her distant love,

safely abstracted from presence.
Elle's goodness found in her forgiving.

("the wayfarer")

One must turn thoughts
to the displacement of a voyage,
cultivate the mind to under-
take travel's long discomfort
and insecurity such as tripping down stairs
as you look up, and adapt the parlance
of malediction and misunderstanding
for the rare day that all goes well
to consider the Way of the Wayfarer.

As you step onto an overlook,
touch the cold rust of guard rail,
and lift eyes to the migration
of whales spouting in a distant iron-gray sea,
you find Luck's on the road with you
this March, the sheer pluck of choosing
to tarry where others find only Wind.
When asked, Were you born happy?
you say, *No, I was not.*

Rather and persistently melancholic.
Yet the treasure of your get-up-and-go,
your grit in the not-giving-up, always
tempers the story you tell on a lark,
maybe to be a bit magical, who knows?—
the one with fairies at the *bottom* of
the garden in the song that broke you
up every time it's so silly—
that you could never finish.

("curtains of darkness")

Where has Elle, vast as horizon, flush,
then reddening, in some ways, furious at sunset—
and plaintively—pulling at the curtains of darkness,
gone?

A gale-wind has cut a swath in trees past the house.
I lean into that guilt, which is loss, golden,
the gloss of evening sun in a scatter of branch
underfoot.

The gate at the end of the garden is cross-hatched,
unpainted wood, and behind it,
a stillness. The pine and birch are filling with
night.

("Elle at sea")

Once I was   myself again   sea-

              farer   I stood excited at

              sun-

                    water breaking and

                                        glist'ning against the bow
My mind wash'd

backward to
              one went before me
                          to sea
~~before~~ me

              whom I'd never known tho'
              her picture   in father's study in my childhood
                                        with her hair pull'd so tight
skin stretch'd and
              mouth a firm line, a little grim

She sail'd
                          west not east, to—   with
              dreams of plenty which

never ~~to find~~ found
only hard work ~~suffering~~ loneliness   I wonder'd how ~~that had~~ she felt
is how
              I ~~feel~~ felt
              am?

72

("the lost labyrinth")

The labyrinth maintained for years

by troth of those who built it

greened fast when they stopped.

Where do you start

to bring it back

when it's gone

       to seed?

     Indeed

the labyrinth's exemplary

of the idiom, its pathway untrod,

its name forgot. Though the forest

grow over it, you might, after all, find

your way if, as is still said, troth's a force.

("the labyrinth of forgiveness")

In the middle of the end she lands.

She'd said *Come* to all of it,

and it all came and now it's all,

as it must be, gone. She never called for help.

She never said "forgive me" to another,

but the language of forgiveness can be silent:

unheard or unspoken.

Forgiveness is a labyrinth, a way,

going this direction and not that,

the ethical route and heart's root,

the *core*, of course, riddle of how

to cure the poison of the demon,

that bitterness which

bent her like a bell

until at last she sounded

sound.

(*"still/*her")

Elle stood in the square wanting to hear the language she was leaving, the desire alive even as the moment passed.

What language can one speak to the dead?

Into the cathedral Elle walked. Onto the labyrinth that she could see among the chairs used to cover it up she stepped. She saw before her letters, columnar glyphs: *words as if in code (Corinth, Kore?)*. Said: *I know my name and yours.*

Yours, she whispered. And, *mine*.

> Elle's hand was being held. She was aware of the touch, that someone was cupping her hand in theirs. Mine, she thought, in the real air, the real hand that was hers, which could be held but would soon be molecules in the world going on without her. No no no NO! The world in which *You* would continue. "She's still *her*," *You* wrote.

She would set a candle now that she was here in the nave, the great stone arches, the stained-glass windows spectraling the light, and *Phantom* playing the spectacular organ.

NOTES

The dedication is to dear friends who died over the two years in which this book was taking shape following the death of my mother: Lynn Wilson, Adrian Oktenberg, Moriah Marston, Maxine Marshall, and L. Evangeline (Erickson) Hogue.

Reading around in the literature about labyrinths, historically and mystically, as well as reading many collections of poetry along the way, I have been moved, sometimes perhaps unconsciously, for I was gathering language like a bricoleur as the poem evolved in fits and starts. I have noted sources as carefully, often long after the fact of having written the section, as possible. Some quotations are so well-known that I thought it unnecessary to cite their sources. Etymological quotations are from the OED. To all those whose works inspired me along the way, all and ever-gratitude.

("a troth"): See C.D. Wright's *One with Others* for an excavation of the beautiful old word, *troth*, and its close connection to *truth*.

("L is for love'"): See the brilliant collection, *L Travels*, by Elisabeth Frost.

("my pilgrimage"), ("*dehors* et *dedans*"), ("the thinking veiling"), ("a spire"), ("the wayfarer"): Portions quoted, translated, paraphrased and riffed on, from Paul Zumthor's *La mesure du monde: Répresentation de l'espace au Moyen Âge*. My thanks to Antoine Gallais-Billaud for the lead to and loan of the book, which remains untranslated into English.

("and to see"): "Love that of erth and se hath governaunce": Chaucer's *Troilus and Criseyde*, paraphrasing the Roman philosopher, Boethius.

("to label something something"): Information and brief quotations/misquotations drawn from the website about the three Black Madonnas at Chartres: http://interfaithmary.net/pages/Chartres.htm.

("Elle tells"): *"Change that"*: An echo of Archbishop Romero's words to the young Carolyn Forché, about to return home after being a Witness for Peace in El Salvador (1978).

("to be-frend"): "good frend": See Lara Vetter's edition of H. D.'s *By Avon River*, which includes the profound study H. D. made of Shakespearean prosody, "Good Frend."

("to walk the labyrinth is amazing"), ("symbolic"), ("cunning"): Information and in some cases direct quotations drawn from "The Mystery of the Great Labyrinth, Chartres Cathedral," by John James. *Studies in Comparative Religion*, 11, 2 (Spring, 1977): http://www.studiesincomparativereligion.com. See also *Chartres: Cathédrale Alchimique et Maçonnique*, by Patrick Burensteinas (Escalquens, France: Éditions Trajectoire, 2012).

("like to a sphere"): I loosely quote from Brian Teare's *Pleasure* (Ahsahta P, 2010), "Of Paradise and the Structure of Gardens." In these lines, Teare himself is quoting Jean Delumeau's *History of Paradise: The Garden of Eden in Myth and Tradition* (Continuum, 1995).

("thinking of *you*"): My thanks to Jonathan Culler for sharing the manuscript of his chapter on the use of apostrophe in the lyric in his book *Theory of the Lyric* (Harvard UP, 2015), which helped me to complete this poem.

("verge"): I am quoting and misquoting Agnes Denes, "Artist's Statement" for a 2003 residency and exhibition at the Samek Art Gallery at Bucknell University. Perhaps obviously, I have edited, cut, and shaped the quotations. My thanks to the artist, and also to then-Gallery Director Dan Mills, for generously including me in some of the events of this residency.

("the labyrinth's experience"): Portions of this section are drawn from information about approaching the Prayer Labyrinth at the St. Francis Renewal Center in Scottsdale, AZ. I've excerpted, collaged and reformatted the Center's pamphlet. My thanks to the poet and singer Pinna Joseph, who walked the Prayer Labyrinth with me, and chanted so movingly upon reaching its center.

("still herself"): For the word "pilgrimly," I draw on the title of Siobhán Scarry's literally marvelous collection, *Pilgrimly* (Parlour Press, 2013), and her poem, "Attempts at Divination," which includes a quotation from Paracelsus in which the term occurs.

("the bitter"): The poem includes slightly misquoted lines from Edna St. Vincent Millay's early poem, "God's World," a favorite of my mother's, and one she requested be read at her funeral.

("Elle at sea"): Erasure poem drawn from my mother's journal about taking the Queen Elizabeth I to England in 1963 to visit her older sister, found among her papers after her death.

("the lost labyrinth"): The story of the lost labyrinth comes from its builder, the poet, Mary Gilliland. Great thanks to Gilliland and her husband, the poet Peter Fortunato, for so generously taking us to the labyrinths at Light on the Hill (not lost, but hard to find!).

("*still* her"): Inspired very tangentially by *The Alphabetic Labyrinth: The Letters in History and Imagination* by Johanna Drucker (Thames and Hudson, 1995), and by my mother's love of language. Also, I was reminded of the phenomenon that truth is revealed in any error when I received my sister's text message from the hospital, where she'd spent the night with our mother in hospice. She wrote, "she's still her," instead of "she's still here." And so, when I arrived, we had just a few more hours with *her*.

BIOGRAPHICAL NOTE

Cynthia Hogue has published thirteen books, including eight collections of poetry, most recently *The Incognito Body* (2006), *Or Consequence* (2010), the co-authored *When the Water Came: Evacuees of Hurricane Katrina* (interview-poems with photographs by Rebecca Ross), published in 2010 in the University of New Orleans Press's Engaged Writers Series, and *Revenance*, listed as one of the 2014 "Standout" books by the Academy of American Poets.

Since 2006, Hogue has been an active translator from contemporary French poetry whose translations have appeared in *American Letters & Commentary, Aufgabe, Interim, Poetry International, APR* and *Field*, among other journals. Her co-authored, book-length translation, *Fortino Sámano (The overflowing of the poem)*, from the French of Virginie Lalucq and Jean-Luc Nancy, was published by Omnidawn in 2012 and won the Harold Morton Landon Translation Award from the Academy of American Poets in 2013. Also known for her criticism, she has published many essays on poetry, ranging from that of Emily Dickinson to Kathleen Fraser and Harryette Mullen. Her critical work includes the co-edited editions *We Who Love To Be Astonished: Experimental Feminist Poetics and Performance Art* (University of Alabama Press, 2001), *Innovative Women Poets: An Anthology of Contemporary Poetry and Interviews* (University of Iowa Press, 2006), and the first edition of H.D.'s *The Sword Went Out to Sea (Synthesis of a Dream), by Delia Alton* (University Press of Florida, 2007).

Among Hogue's honors are an NEA Fellowship in poetry, the H.D. Fellowship at the Beinecke Library at Yale University, a MacDowell Colony residency, and the Witter Bynner Translation Fellowship at the Santa Fe Art Institute. Hogue served as the Distinguished Visiting Writer at Cornell University in the spring of 2014. She was a 2015 NEA Fellow in Translation, and holds the Maxine and Jonathan Marshall Chair in Modern and Contemporary Poetry at Arizona State University.

CPSIA information can be obtained
at www.ICGtesting.com
Printed in the USA
BVOW08s1231130317
478372BV00002B/4/P